Cursive Writing the Easy Way

Barbara Pieper Walding

Steve Catlett
Cover

Cursive Writing the Easy Way

This book is written to provide information and motivation to readers. Its purpose is not to render any type of psychological, legal, or professional advice of any kind. The content is the sole opinion and expression of the author, and not necessarily that of the publisher.

Copyright © 2023 by Barbara Pieper Walding.

All rights reserved. No part of this book may be reproduced, transmitted, or distributed in any form by any means, including, but not limited to, recording, photocopying, or taking screenshots of parts of the book, without prior written permission from the author or the publisher. Brief quotations for noncommercial purposes, such as book reviews, permitted by Fair Use of the U.S. Copyright Law, are allowed without written permissions, as long as such quotations do not cause damage to the book's commercial value. For permissions, write to the publisher, whose address is stated below.

Printed in the United States of America.

ISBN   978-1-64552-179-2   (Paperback)
ISBN   978-1-64552-180-8   (Digital)

Lettra Press books may be ordered through booksellers or by contacting:

Lettra Press LLC
30 N Gould St. Suite 4753
Sheridan, WY 82801
1 307-200-3414 | info@lettrapress.com
www.lettrapress.com

Table of Contents

Introduction 1

Learn Cursive Writing 2

Let's Get Started 3

Directions For All The Letters 4

Group 1 The Upswing Letters 5

Group 2 The Tall Upswing Letters 9

Group 3 The Slanted Oval Letters 12

Group 4 The Hump Letters 15

Normal Sizing 18

Capital Letters 20

Congratulations 43

Introduction

August 2017

I have never tried to publish a book before. I have a BS and MS in education. I have almost 30 years of elementary school teaching, and I just love cursive writing. It is so much more intellectual and romantic.

Some people say it is becoming a lost art, but I don't think so. If it is a lost art, I want to revive it in my own little way.

When I was teaching, my students were recognized in the next grade. The teachers could always spot which students came from me because of their handwriting.

I realize that teachers have to prepare students for testing, so cursive writing is put on the back burner. I don't want this love to die because there is no time for it and because technology has taken over. There is a place for cursive writing in our culture.

This program can be used in elementary through high school. It can be used in home schooling, by parents helping their children in writing, by tutors and small groups. This simple technique can be easily adapted for teens and adults. It is easy enough for some older students to teach themselves.

The San Antonio Express News on Monday, February 27, 2017 had an article on the editorial page written by Katrina Erickson entitled "cursive plays vital role in success". It was written primarily for Texas schools. She gives many reasons why cursive writing should be in the curriculum of every school district because it brings success to students in many ways. Maybe I am on to something.

I think students will find this method unique and appealing. They will feel good about themselves to know this writing form.

Learn Cursive Writing

There are 3 differences between manuscript (printing) and cursive writing.

1. The letters and words are slanted.

2. The letters are connected in words.

3. The letters "i" and "j" are dotted and the "t" and "x" are crossed after you have written the letter or word.

Cursive writing is like art. It is beautiful and shows you are intelligent and well-educated.

Just think, you will be able to write your own name. You can write your grandma a thank you note in cursive writing.

She will be thrilled.

When you get older you can write your signature on your driver's license application and then on your license.

Imagine going to the store and writing a check.

You will be able to use this new skill in many ways.

Let's Get Started

We will write larger than usual because you are just beginning and need to get the feel of the letter. The slant some people think is hard, but it's just a a little trick. In manuscript the paper is straight in front of you like this.

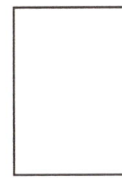

To get the slant all you have to do is turn your paper like this if you are right handed,

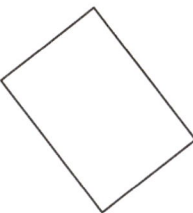

or like this if you are left-handed.

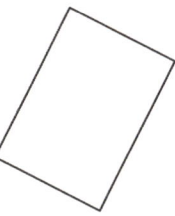

Place the bottom triangle facing your belly button. That's the trick. You will write straight up and down. When you are finished writing, just turn the paper straight again. Hooray! You have your slant. It's not much of a trick is it?

With your other hand, hold the paper at the top. That way the paper won't slip and slide.

Directions For All The Letters

1. Look for the dot . because this is where you begin.

2. Look for the number in front of the letter which tells you how many strokes there are. You never stop in the middle of a stroke - just finish the stroke.

3. Trace the letter to see how it feels.

4. Write the letter in the air as many times as you need to get the feel of the letter.

5. When you think you've "got it", trace over the first letter again.

6. Now write a whole line of the letter.

7. Circle what you think is your best letter.

You can do these 7 steps no matter what letter you are writing.

Group 1 The Upswing Letters

Look for the dot. to begin.

(3). *i*

Remember to dot the "i" last and count it as a stroke.

(2). *e*

(3). *w*

(4). *w*

Notice the hook at the end - the last stroke.

(3). *s*

(4).

This is the sliding chair letter because if you sat on this chair, you would fall off.

(4). j

Now that you can write some letters, let's see if you can write some words using these letters. Here are a few examples. There is another step in connecting letters. They know how to share. The last stroke of the letter and the first stroke of the second letter must share. It sounds complicated, but it's really not. Let's take a look.

is

Can you see the connection? Trace over it. I hope you can see it because it is very important. We learn to share in life, and so do our words in cursive writing. Copy these words to get some practice.

sue

sir

Don't fall off the chair.

rise

we

(Notice the unusual connection here.)

wee

sure

wise

were

Group 2 The Tall Upswing Letters

We will use two spaces because we are just learning. They begin the same way as the up swingers do. Some of these letters will go below the line. Watch carefully and don't forget to draw the letters in the air.

(2). *t*

(3). *b*

(4). *f*

(3). *h*

(4). *h*

This letter looks like a preying mantis.

(4). *p*

Notice the third stroke goes backwards.

(3). *t*

Notice that the first stroke doesn't go up to the top line like the other tall letters do. It only goes part way.

Let's make some words. Now we have two groups from which to choose. Remember the connections.

blue

feet

kiss

Remember to dot the i at the end.

pill

rust

hire

Can you think of other words using the two groups of letters?

Group 3 The Slanted Oval Letters

Make the oval slanted first. It is all one stroke.

(2) *a*

(2) *d*

(3) *g*

(2) *o*

This is the pig's tail letter because it curls like a pig's tail at the end.

(3) *g*

(4) *q*

Look at the difference between g & q. Look at Stroke 3 in g. It goes backward. Now look at Stroke 3 in q. It goes forward. This is the same as in manuscript.

Remember the seven steps to writing in cursive.
Review them if you forgot.
Now let's write some words using letters from all 3 groups.

date

quiet

later

table

rose

shirt

coat

wish

Group 4 The Hump Letters

(3). *m*

(2). *n*

(2). *x*

You can cross the X going backwards at the end.

(3). *y*

(2). *v*

(3). *y*

Let's write some words with group 4 letters.

mame

zoo

very

xray

vase

main

Now you know how to write all the 26 lowercase letters. You can write all your spelling words in cursive and amaze your teacher.

By the way, it is faster to write in cursive than in manuscript.

Normal Sizing

In reality we don't write this large. It's just for learning and practice. Now look at the normal size for writing the 26 letters and words.

Trace the letters and words in the normal size. Get the feel of each. The letters and words are the same as those we have been practicing.

i e u w s r j

is sir rise we were

l b f h k p t

blue feel kill pill

a d c q g o

date quite later table rose wish

m n x y v z

name zoo very vase

Capital Letters

Congratulations! You have now graduated to capital letters

You will now be able to write your name and even the name of your school. Many of the capital letters do not connect to other letters in the word. Sometimes it will be your own choice.

Let's start with most of the letters that begin the same way - the candy cane letters. Some may be a little difficult to write, but you can do it.

(3) *M*

Notice that the m and n go downhill.

Mary

(3) *N*

Nora

(3) *H*

This letter has 2 parts that you connect . part 1 ⟩ part 2 ✗

Henry

K

Part 1 ⟩ part 2 ⟨ Put the two parts together.

Karen

(2) *Q* — Almost like the number 2

Quentin

(2) *V*

Vera

(3) *U*

Ulysses

(4) *W*

Walter

Cross the T last.

(2) *X*

Has two parts an upside-down 6 and a regular 6.

Xavier

Cross the X last.

(3) *Y*

Yolanda

(3) *Z*

Zachary

These letters look like the lowercase letters and are the easiest to write.

(2) *U*

(2) *O*

Notice the pig's tail again.

Andrea

Otto

Start in the middle letters

(4) *R*

Retrace the downward stroke up in all these letters.

(3) *P*

(5) *B*

Notice the boat

Robert

Paul

Betty

------- Backward beginning letters

(3) *I*

Notice the boat

(3) *J*

Both the letters start backwards

Isaac

John

These letters start with a loop going backward.

(2) *E*

(2) *C*

Evan

Carl

(2) *L*

Remember Laverne and Shirley?

Laverne

(3) *D*

The fat belly letter! Hope you can see why. It also has a pig's tail.

David

Daniel

Remember to dot the i.. Notice the pig's tail.

---------- Two upswing letters combined with boats ---

(4)

(3)

Grace

Susan

These letters are in two parts. You may connect them or leave them in two parts. It is your choice. You make the top part first and then have fun making the bottom part. Notice they also end in boats.

(3) *j̇*

or

(3) *j̇*

(4) *j̇*

or

(4) *j̇*

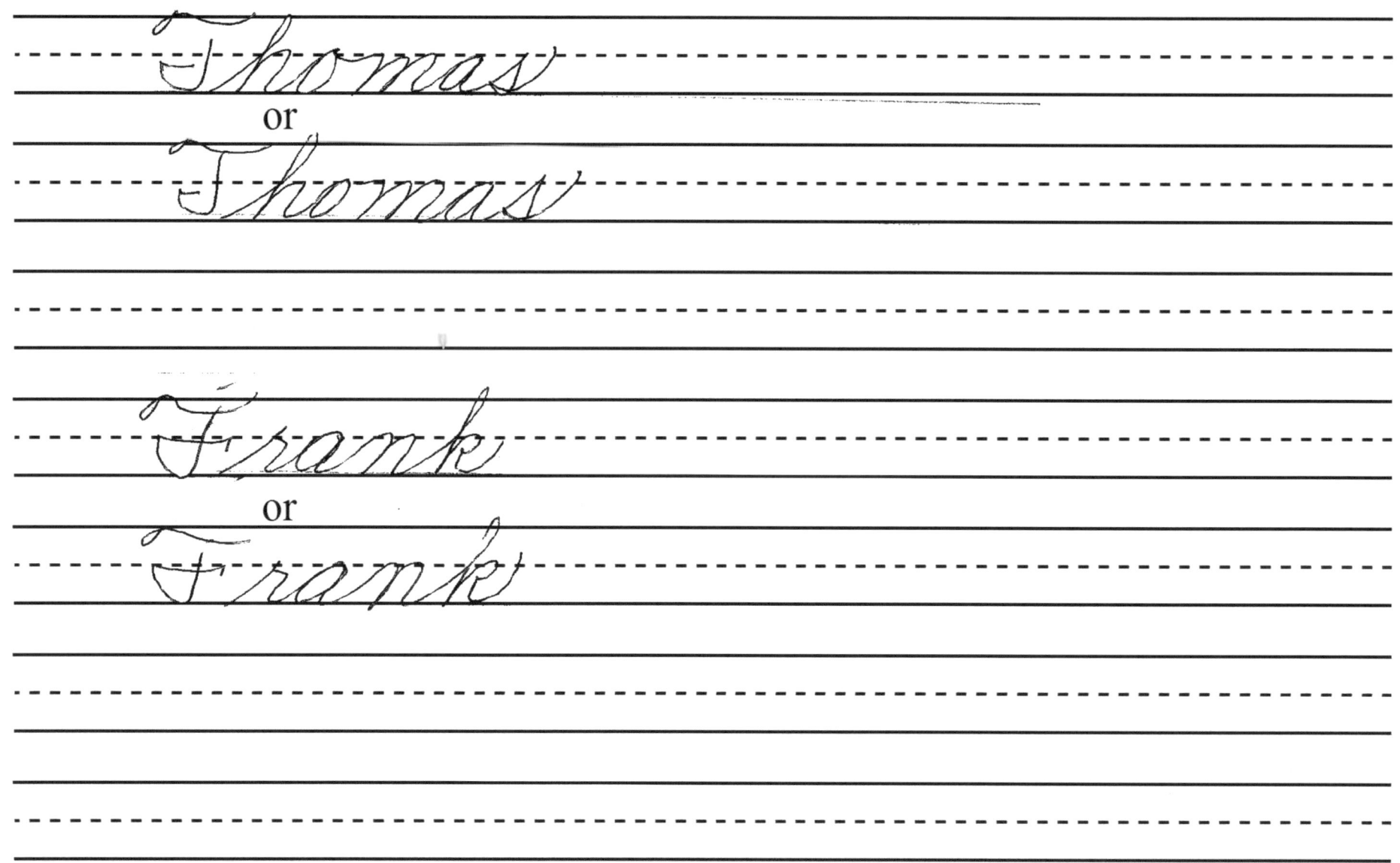

Extra Practice Pages

Andrea

Otto

Robert

Paul

Betty

Isaac

John

Karen

Walter

Xavier

Yolanda

Zachary

Thomas

Frank

Mary

Nora

Henry

Ken

Quentin

Vera

Ulysses

Evan

Carl

Laverne

David

Grace

Here are those names written in a normal style

Andrea

Otto

Robert

Paul

Betty

Isaac

Mary

Nora

Henry

Ken

Quentin

Vera

Ulysses

John

Evan

Carl

Laverne

David

Grace

Susan

Karen

Walter

Xavier

Yolanda

Zachary

Thomas

Frank

Thomas

Frank

Numbers

Numbers can also be written in cursive writing. Remember when we slanted the paper to get slanted letters. It's easy to slant numbers the same way. Just turn the paper pointed towards your belly button and write straight.

1234567890

1234567890 Now isn't that easy?

This extra page is for you to write your friend's names.

Now you are an expert in cursive writing!

Congratulations!

www.ingramcontent.com/pod-product-compliance
Lightning Source LLC
Chambersburg PA
CBHW041150070526
44583CB00004B/138